Ten Steps to a More Joyful Relationship with Food

Sal Dhalla

The Food Witch

Illustrations by Harry Bird

ISBN 978-1-8380613-0-2 (paperback)
ISBN 978-1-8380613-1-9 (Kindle)
ISBN 978-1-8380613-2-6 (ePub)

Every effort has been made to ensure that the information in this book was correct at press time, and the author does not assume and hereby disclaims any liability to any party for loss, damage, or disruption caused by errors or omissions, whether the result of negligence, accident, or any other cause. This book is not intended to replace medical advice or the recommendations of clinicians. If you plan to make lifestyle changes, especially relating to diet or exercise, it is at your own risk and medical advice should be sought prior to doing so. The contents of this book are offered as a personal story, opinion and information, and do not guarantee any specific results or outcome.

Illustrations by Harry Bird.

Cover design by Laylah Garner.

CONTENTS

ACKNOWLEDGEMENTS

Thanks to my mum and my grandma for all their food-based inspiration. Ian for his welcome nagging and advice, Caroline (head witch) and Harry for his amazing illustrations. And of course, to all my friends and family with whom I have formed and shared my love of food and all the memories and experiences that lie behind what I do.

INTRODUCTION

Our relationship with food is at once extremely personal and heavily influenced by external factors. Through the lens of what I have learnt through life coaching and my personal relationship with and love for food, I hope to share my perspective on what having a 'good' or 'healthy' or 'positive' relationship with food really means. That it is largely about mindset and internal work rather than doing the things to change our external or physical selves that we all often think will offer us validation. I am not a nutritionist or dietician, and this is now an increasingly deliberate feature of what I do. My work and passion centres on our intuitive and spiritual relationship with food, particularly through cooking. And I believe that our bodies and our intuition are wise and sensitive enough to tell us what we need when we need it, and to ride out the waves of imperfect nutrition—without the need for restrictive diets, calorie counting, dwelling on macronutrients or tricking your body into silencing the physical and mental signals associated with appetite and fullness. Unfortunately, there is a huge multi-billion dollar global industry based on promoting the very things I have just said I think are unnecessary (in fact, counterproductive) to having a joyful relationship with food.

To be honest, I had always taken my relationship with food for granted, to the point that it took me a really long time to even see it as something special and relatively unique to me—let alone something worthwhile sharing with others. I find it pretty easy to have a joyful experience with food (although I haven't always been good at reflecting that back on my relationship with myself: I have worked on and continue to work on improving this), it's definitely a loving, passionate and abundant relationship and it comes really naturally to me. Realising that it's far from that easy for most other people, I decided to focus my career on changing that. In particular, I direct my efforts at the great majority of people in the middle of the pack—not those with eating disorders or weight-related health problems, or severe food restrictions driven by medical needs. But the crowd of people who aren't at the extremes of a relationship with food, those with busy lives, jobs, families, financial constraints, stress, pressure and competition for time and resources—people whose relationship with food is either purely functional and joyless or a daily battle over body image and weight through both diet and lifestyle, without it tipping over into a clinical diagnosis. And for that reason, I deliberately wanted to produce something short, sweet and easily digestible (I will never apologise for my puns!).

Our relationship with food can be pretty complicated. Western society is in the grip of diet culture, to the point that we are ingrained with the belief that there is a moral value attached to our weight, specifically the greater moral value of thinness (thinness being automatically equated with health), and that the sole aim of our relationship with food should be to achieve moral validation through thinness. It creates a fearful, negative mindset around food that has us swiping our credit cards with abandon at the promise of finally solving this problem. So, if you are reading this because you think it will give you weight loss tools, I promise you that it won't. But I hope that won't stop you from reading on, because what you will find is a number of ways you can reorient your relationship with food towards joy, pleasure and freedom, and start to break the conditioning that makes you link what you eat to your sense of value and self-worth. You may have lifelong views challenged, you may need to ask yourself some difficult questions—but in pursuit of something that we all deserve, a great relationship with food and with ourselves. In any case, this is about coming from a mindset of self-love, joy, intuition and abundance.

1

SAY NO TO DIET CULTURE

This is the big one—and one you really have to go for so that the rest of this book makes sense. Diet culture is a societal and often subconscious belief system that being thin is equivalent to being morally virtuous, healthy and generally better than everyone else. It offers body image ideals that are unrealistic and imposes the belief that people that don't achieve them have less worth and are somehow inferior, damaged and unhealthy. It's the voice in your head that tells you that you're fat and that your body shape will stop you from being happy, getting a job or finding love, so you must do everything you can to change it to fit the ideal you are being given to compare yourself to.

Diet culture promotes low-level disordered eating amongst huge sections of the population, and whilst this has always affected women disproportionately, its impact on men is not to be ignored. It's an industry that was valued at just under $190 BN in 2018 (Research and Markets, 2019) and is in large part playing on the patriarchal, capitalist, fear-based mindset that convinces us we have no idea what's good for us or how to feed ourselves, so we need someone else to do it for us, or tell us how to (and get paid for it). Or that we are too busy with our jobs and responsibilities to feed or exercise ourselves properly, so we need someone else to do it for us or tell us how to (and get paid for it). And if we don't, we will die miserable, alone, poor and fat. And it doesn't relate to the reality of food in the modern world. The morally superior, effortlessly thin, clean-eating people you are told to emulate live a lifestyle and eat a diet that bears no resemblance to what real lives look like, or what is on offer in the shops and markets the majority of people buy their food at. Yet you are 'expected' to end up looking like that anyway.

Spotting this extremely pervasive toxic culture can be really hard, especially because we have all grown up with it and had it drilled into us from a young age, however subtly and subconsciously. Our mothers handed down fears about self-worth and body image when they innocently and unthinkingly commented on our weight loss or gain. Our friends make us feel like better people for being thinner when they say, 'You look great, have you lost weight?'. We automatically use words like 'fat' to describe how we feel when we have gained weight or had a big meal, deepening the stigma attached to what is just a word. We demonise hunger, trying to distract ourselves, feeling frustrated at our bodies for needing food when we have more 'important' things to do, and seeking ways to avoid the feeling in the first place. Anything that equates food or body shape with morality or suggests weight-loss should be the primary goal of your lifestyle choices is diet culture. It's impossible to really love food or yourself if you subscribe to that belief system.

It can be a thorny issue, particularly when you start calling the world and the people in it up on their diet culture promotion. But dieting is, at the end of the day, a huge commercial goldmine, creating and then preying on fears that go right to people's sense of self-worth and societal value. And it's so insidious and pervasive that it's easy to miss it, or not think it's that big of a deal, and then eventually it's in your subconscious and ruling the way you live your life. So, step one, let's agree to say no to diet culture and stop it dominating our lives, thoughts and eating habits. I'm not saying it's a click of the fingers, easy kind of thing. It's generations of subconscious conditioning that needs to be worked out consciously. But as with many things, just knowing and calling it for what it is takes the sting out of it. So start with spotting diet culture, then consciously choosing not to let it take up room in your brain. It's going to free up a lot of headspace to fill with the proactive and positive steps I'm about to share with you so that you can turn this story of fear into one of love and joy.

Social media is probably our most plentiful source of diet culture at the moment and is one you can at least curate, if not control. Be ruthless. If people or businesses you follow start promoting faddy eating habits or restrictions, link being unhealthy or inferior with weight, offer ways to lose weight (no matter what they are) in return for money, then they are part of diet culture and you have no need for that in your life. Unfollow, unfollow, unfollow. Fill your feed with things that bring you joy, positivity and inspiration. Don't spend ages scrolling and comparing yourself to others (whether it's body image, money, clothes, family life)—just as you can curate what you see online, your profile and others' are also a carefully filtered and selected version of that person and bear limited resemblance to reality. If you ever need reminding of that, look at your own Instagram page and see how much of your own life you filter. And you can make it work for you. I fill my Instagram with positivity, motivation, affirmation and tasty food. And if something doesn't tick one of those boxes and promotes beliefs or conditioning that I have worked to free myself from, I just hit that lovely unfollow button (or mute if you want to be politely British about it).

Diet culture doesn't just make us believe that thin people are morally and physically superior. It also assigns moral attributes to specific foods and food groups. The demonisation of carbs, sugar or fat, for example. Calling foods 'good' or 'bad'; cheat foods and cheat days; guilt-free food whatever that is meant to be. Even the words 'healthy' and 'unhealthy' or 'clean' and 'dirty' have taken on such powerful characteristics that they have lost real meaning in our lives. They now carry such weight that we believe we should only eat healthy things. But healthy means something that is good for your health, actively benefitting it. And conversely unhealthy is something that doesn't actively contribute to or benefit your health. But why does that mean unhealthy foods can never be eaten? Why is the focus so singularly on how food affects our physical bodies? What about pleasure and joy and satisfaction? Of course, on the whole, you want to balance it out by mainly eating healthy foods, but that doesn't mean that including unhealthy things in your diet is actively *bad* for you or more importantly, *makes you a bad person*. Because it doesn't. And this mindset makes us fearful of lots of different foods and groups of foods, and we have more than enough stuff to worry about and be fearful of without having to include what we eat on that list.

And all of this is true both in public and private. We are all guilty of commenting on each other's bodies, exclaiming about our size, shape, fullness or feelings of 'fatness'. It's just as important to watch how we speak to others as it is how we speak to ourselves. Also in this category is how we speak about others when they aren't around, or if they are people we don't know. Again, this is something we all do so automatically and subconsciously that we probably don't even notice we do it. But, 'X has gotten SO fat' said behind someone's back or about a celebrity may not directly hurt the person you are talking about, but it does suggest you attach moral value to body size, to the person you say it to. Worst of all, it suggests that you attach moral value to body size to *yourself*. Similarly, don't praise yourself or others for losing weight. You and your loved ones have far more interesting and beautiful facets to them than that, and you have a wealth of things to choose from to compliment them about—things that have nothing to do with their weight, body size or eating habits.

Rather than giving food binary characteristics or moral value, I prefer to think of it in terms that relate to how I feel or how food makes me feel—and this helps to foster a more loving and intuitive relationship with food and my body. In fact, I actively try to avoid using the words 'healthy' and 'unhealthy' not because they are inaccurate but because they are so loaded with stigma and moral judgement that we all interpret them and are affected by hearing them differently. Instead, I frame my food choices with words like satisfying, energising, refreshing, comforting, exciting, interesting, wholesome, nourishing, indulgent, vitalising. And when I want something comforting, I may go for a hearty vegetable stew, but equally, I may go for sweet and creamy rice pudding. Either way, I'm comforted and without moral judgement from within (or without, because I ignore it). And at no point do I ascribe relative value to things based on where they rank on the healthy scale. Their value is in satisfying my hunger, fuelling my body and bringing me sensory pleasure and joy through cooking and eating, and that's it.

2

CHOICE INSTEAD OF RESTRICTION

Food restriction is another big hitter when we look at the obstacles to having a joyful relationship with food. It has a huge psychological and physical impact on how we think about what we eat and the way we deal with our hunger, cravings and the idiosyncrasies of our bodies. Obviously, if you have an allergy or a medical condition that is an important exception and please keep avoiding the foods that make you clinically unwell. But the point I am trying to get across here is that you can eat well and increase the proportion of whole and fresh foods in your life without applying restrictions to your diet. Dieting and restriction put you in a mindset of fear and scarcity which is not conducive to having an intuitive, life-affirming relationship with food.

First of all, eating is a basic need that is required for our bodies to continue to function. Just like drinking, going to the toilet, or sleeping. We wouldn't think of denying our thirst or bladder signals to the point of feeling awful. If you need to pee, you pee. If you're thirsty, you drink something. Yet so many people don't approach hunger in the same way: they try to distract themselves from a natural signal their body is giving them. Or drink water instead of eating, in case it's actually thirst masquerading as hunger. Or wait until an arbitrarily specified time to eat. And equally, we wouldn't only allow ourselves a limited number of trips to the toilet in a day or restrict our water intake to below what our body needs to function. We drink and go to the toilet when we need to, trusting the signals our body sends us and responding to them intuitively. All too often we don't treat our hunger with the same respect.

The fitness and wellness industries also encourage us to restrict our food, and it doesn't stop at earning your food through exercise (see Chapter 4)—cheat days are a great example of arbitrary restriction and food-driven morality. Eating any food of any kind at any time for any reason isn't cheating. Unless you're actually cheating in a competitive eating contest. The very use of the word 'cheat' creates negative associations with the foods you eat on those days regardless of what they may be. And somehow we can be persuaded, through fear of ending up fat and unloved, that we will weigh less if we eat a piece of cake on Sunday instead of Wednesday.

Restriction messes with your mind in a multitude of ways. Firstly, it makes you want the things that are off-limits even more. Secondly, it creates a cycle of negative self-talk and self-judgement around certain foods—even just wanting them, let alone eating them. Thirdly, your ability to exercise moderation goes out of the window when you let the restrictions go, and this is both conscious ('In for a penny, in for a pound', etc.) and subconscious ('Who knows when these foods will be available again, better eat as much as possible regardless of fullness.'). So how can you turn this around and make it work for you? Consider replacing restriction with choice.

I don't consciously force myself to restrict my diet in any way. But that doesn't mean what I eat hasn't changed radically as I have embarked on my journey of intuition and self-development. The more I prioritise my well-being and loving myself unconditionally, the more I have been able to make food a force for feeling great in life: mind, body and soul. It all happened by stealth and without forethought or force, upon reflection, it mirrored my self-development journey quite closely. And even now that I basically don't eat any meat, I deliberately don't call myself a vegetarian (more on that in a moment). As someone who has never dieted or obsessed about my nutrition or weight, I feel like an outside observer to much of diet culture and it all appears like disordered eating to me. And don't get me wrong, I know I'm incredibly lucky to have no guilt issues around food, and I understand how damaging it can be for so many people. I know because I have struggled with guilt issues about pretty much everything else, and have seen loved ones battle with eating disorders first hand. Food is the only area of my life where guilt has never seemed to crop up. I make food choices more and more out of love for myself and really trying to understand what I need physically, mentally and emotionally. I *choose* not to eat meat because I feel better in all those respects, and I know in my gut it's the right thing for me (almost all the time).

Let's take a non-controversial one. Vegetables. More vegetables in your life is a good thing, agreed? And yes, if you go vegetarian or vegan you will definitely eat less meat, and hopefully (but not necessarily, and this is important to remember) eat more vegetables too. But speaking from experience, the moment I called myself a vegetarian, I was consumed with an unreasonable and seemingly permanent craving for a juicy, meat and cheese-laden hamburger. Literally every time I thought about food, I would think about that burger. Maybe if it was breakfast time—a bacon sandwich. It was ridiculous and consuming. Particularly because by the time I gave meat up I was hardly eating it anyway. As a food lover I only wanted the best meat, and as I became more aware of environmental issues wanted to have the highest welfare most ethically produced meat I could find. It got to the point where I would eat beef when the raw milk traders at the markets I was running my business at had an old dairy cow that they used for meat. So, once every 3-4 months, if that (which was fine, because that was probably all I could afford!). Part of the reason I decided not to eat meat anymore was that I was connecting to my body and intuition in a more general sense (as part of a difficult but life-changing year of working with an amazing life and business coach, Caroline Britton who is an absolute witch!), and I became acutely aware of how I felt physically when I ate meat. Yet restricting it had such a psychological impact on me that all of this conscious thinking and doing went out of the window, and I craved meat in ways I never had before. The big test then came on a trip to New York for a wedding, where I promptly discovered being a vegetarian was not particularly easy, and definitely not fun. Options were limited and usually of the super faddy overly healthy raw and tasteless variety. All the good stuff had meat in it. I forgot that it's the sort of place where even vegetable side dishes can't escape a smattering of bacon. And it was no fun for me. So, I decided to go with the flow and eat the things that seemed most delicious and appealing rather than sticking to a restriction that was making my trip less joyful. And I really enjoyed the rest of the trip and the food I ate. I was more aware of how it impacted my body but was also consciously able to take responsibility for that decision and live with the very much temporary outcome (I was bloated, and my system slowed *way* down, but I got over it pretty quickly with some veggies).

When I got back home after that trip all I really wanted to do was eat fresh veggies, whole grains and fruit. And that's what I did. A few weeks later, I went out for dinner to a place I had been keen to try, and they had sold out of a few of the vegetarian dishes. Rather than not eat enough and be disappointed in this place I was so excited to be at (and the food was delicious, by the way), we just ordered a couple of yummy sounding meat dishes to make up the meal. Around this time, I decided to remove this seemingly innocuous 'vegetarian' label and restriction from my diet and to reframe it as positive and affirmative choices that I am free to make, change and change back depending on how I feel mind, body and soul. And I promise you, this hasn't meant that I have become a regular meat-eater again. I am basically a vegetarian who eats vegan a lot of the time and has a few bites of meat on the odd occasion. But inwardly, I let myself eat without restriction, and just happen to make the choice not to eat meat most of the time. If you made me assess it, I probably eat vegan at least half the time and eat small amounts of meat so infrequently I couldn't quantify it. One last story on this. Last Christmas it was left to me to carve the roast rib of beef, and my mum was so proud of her work and kind of begging me to eat some. It looked incredible, and as I carved it, I felt compelled to enjoy that chef's perk—the most delicious, caramelised bits of meat from the edges and scraps. So, I put a few morsels in my mouth. They were heavenly. And when it came to dinner, with all the veggies and potatoes and Yorkshire puddings on my plate I chose to eat those things, having enjoyed the taste of the beef I had already had, and knowing that eating more wasn't worth how I would feel after. At the same meal, I chose to eat the meat, and then not to. It completely changes your relationship with food: empowering you to make choices that make your body feel great but also allowing you to take responsibility for enjoying foods that provide pleasure and joy beyond the realm of nutrition, without judgement or guilt. And I'm definitely not saying eating more vegetables and less or no meat can't be part of an ethical and sustainable relationship with food that is also joyful. Part of what brings me joy about eating close to no meat is that it is kinder to the planet, and if by making a choice to be more ethical in your eating you get joy, then include that as part of the 'more' too.

So, don't focus on not eating certain foods or restricting what you can eat when. Don't impose limits, give yourself choices. Don't restrict, decide. Don't forbid things like meat or cheese, just choose to eat vegetables instead because they energise and nourish you. You can achieve the same outcome in a way that is much more joyful and kinder to yourself and helps to reprogramme your mindset when it comes to food.

3

ACCEPT AND KNOW YOUR BODY

Whilst I ultimately believe it's possible to love your body unconditionally, just accepting it can be a powerful first step. Acceptance is infinitely better than hating your body, and an entry point to getting to know it, appreciating it, eventually becoming grateful for (and even loving) it. Instead of focusing on ourselves, however, we are frequently driven to comparison and feelings of inferiority—hating our bodies for not looking like the images we see on social media, rather than appreciating them for all that they do. There is a section on gratitude later, but the headline is, you can't hate something if you're grateful for it (even the 'bad' stuff that happens to you).

Our bodies are amazing, just as they are—by the very fact that they do all the things we need them to do just to survive (breathing, eating, drinking etc.). They can do those things so automatically or intuitively that we can take them for granted and then use our minds and bodies to do all sorts of other awesome, unique and amazing things. By starting to appreciate all that our bodies do for us and how much we continue to demand (and receive) from them, we also start to connect more to how our body feels and responds to the care (or lack of) that we offer it. I came at it from a slightly roundabout way—I have always had a good relationship with food but for a long time I largely ignored my body, took it for granted and did the minimum required to maintain it to get me through the days of my miserable neon-lit corporate existence.

In particular, I never set out to improve my relationship with food or my body. My self-development journey involved a lot of internal work centred around how I saw myself, how I was ruled by fear and ego, and how I was caught up in a 'should' and fear-based mindset. I worked on reconnecting to my intuition, figuring out what I found meaningful in life and strived very hard to learn to love myself and own my gift, so that I could have the courage and constitution to be successful in my chosen vocation. As a happy bonus of this, my relationship with food and my body also changed quite radically and unexpectedly, almost as soon as I started to live more intuitively and prioritise my needs, desires and self-care. And it was literally as simple as no longer ignoring the signals my body gave me (about anything) and not letting my rational, logical brain take the charge on decisions that really should have been driven by physical and intuitive signs. I became acutely aware of how eating meat made me feel and have more or less stopped eating it (as you know, except for the odd occasion when the joy and pleasure aspect of eating meat are a worthwhile trade-off). I started to realise my restlessness and anxiety later in the day was linked to how much movement or time outside I got. I became less able to delay eating even if I was convinced I had more 'important' things to do. Now, if I'm hungry, I'm immediately so unproductive and annoying, I know that I need to eat, no matter how early or late it is, regardless of how little work

I have or have not done up until that point in the day. There are days now that I don't start working until after lunch—if I need to sleep later, I do, if it's a nice morning I may walk my dogs in the sunshine. I journal and have my coffee; I may exercise first. Then inevitably I eat something. And it may be 1 p.m. before I turn on the computer, and I may only work for six hours that day, but they will be productive. In the past, I would have thought this was lazy and stupid, but now I'm sure that if I had turned the computer on at 9 a.m. instead and forced myself to sit in front of it, I would have produced nothing of value by 1 p.m. and would likely be so tense, hungry (*hangry*) and useless by that point that I would have had to have eaten something anyway, only to finally be a productive person at 2 or 3 p.m. and probably only end up fitting in four or five hours of useful work, despite having spent ten sitting at my desk. Now, by appreciating the fact that my intuition and my body know what I need far better than my ego-driven, externally conditioned brain, I can be more productive in less time.

Back to the point. Knowing, respecting and caring for your body goes far beyond food, it's also about sleep, movement, social interaction, rest, play, hydration, mindfulness, self-development. It's about being aware of how all the aspects of your self-care and routine affect you: mind, body and soul—and then setting up your life to maximise the good feelings you get from those things. It's not self-indulgent, living your best life is about being productive and useful too. And sure stuff gets in the way, but it won't do as much if you see self-care as a priority, a joy and a requirement for you to be the most productive and of service version of yourself you can be—instead of a chore that gets in the way of work or responsibilities. 'You can't pour from an empty cup', is one of my favourite affirmative phrases here, and it's so true, particularly when it comes to food. In a physical sense as well as a spiritual one—you need the fuel, the lifeforce and the joy of good food, feeling well fed and being sustained to be that awesome person you are.

As I mentioned at the start of this section and will elaborate on later, this is a great area to work into your gratitude (and appreciation) practice. You can definitely appreciate your body, even just for getting you through the day—and you may scoff at me for suggesting it, but see it for the amazing feat of nature and nurture that it is, and you may start to genuinely look at your body in a different light.

4

JOYFUL MOVEMENT

I don't see exercise and eating as a trade-off, yet diet culture promotes the idea that we need to earn the food we eat by exercising. Instead of looking at it that way, I see them as two complementary aspects of my human experience and self-care, and as part of the fuel and energy I give my body to do what it needs to do. I don't exercise out of obligation or fear of getting fat, I do it because it makes me feel strong, vital and energised, and because it's fundamental to my mood, mental wellbeing and sleep quality. Creating fear around exercise is just another way diet culture is seeping into our mindset. We don't need to exercise to permit ourselves to eat or indulge. But finding movement that is enjoyable and makes you feel good physically, mentally and emotionally is not only great for how you feel about yourself, but it can also help to break the subconscious association between food and exercise. You're doing it because you want to, not because you want to eat.

Why make exercise a punishment you have to endure so that

you can eat certain foods that you like? Food is food, movement is movement. They are both amazing, pleasurable and can make you feel great, and are important for a happy and fulfilled existence. One doesn't require the other, but you *do* require them both. You are far easier prey if you fear that everything you eat is going to add directly to your waistline, and you will do (and pay for) things that you don't even enjoy a little bit. Things that actively make you feel miserable and that you dread doing. Now that I've stopped doing those things in all areas of my life, I am appalled at how much of our lives we live accepting that we have to do things that make us genuinely miserable.

It has taken me a long time to figure out what sort of movement I find joyful but now that I have, it's astounding to me how much exercise I actually *want* to do. For years I never did any meaningful regular exercise (probably from the age of 18-30 at least) and never really felt I needed to, particularly because I wasn't worried about my weight or body size. Yes, I was viewing losing weight as the only driver for exercising. Oops. And actually, in that mindset, I found it really hard to exercise consistently. I didn't want to go to the gym or run as I hated doing them both. I was too tired, busy and self-important, and under too much pressure to take time out for self-care. And I didn't care if my weight fluctuated due to my lifestyle and diet, and it never did that much. So, throughout my twenties, I was not big in size, but not fit or vital. Definitely not prioritising self-care, definitely suffering enough at work and in my miserable social existence not to add on the sufferance of exercise, which was all I saw it as.

But once I found something I enjoyed and got mental and emotional benefits from, I became able to determine when I needed to move to maintain or shift my energy. It started with indoor bouldering. I felt the need to dust off my creaky entering mid-thirties joints and muscles, and it was at the start of what turned out to be a massive surge in the popularity and availability of the sport (at least before the 2020 global pandemic). It seemed to involve a fair amount of coffee, cake, chatting to cool people and sitting on the floor, with the odd bit of climbing in between— so it was a pretty approachable way to start moving. And the bug bit me hard. It was fun, accessible, easy to progress and get better, incredibly rewarding, satisfying, and sociable, but also a great solo activity. You are constantly pushing the limits of your strength, your nerve and your belief in yourself. Every time I got to the top of the wall I felt like a superhero. And I still do. It was the remedy I needed for my anxiety and self-doubt. Honestly, it completely changed my life and my lifestyle, as well as physical changes (which were never the primary aim). And once I started climbing regularly and trying to connect to my body and intuition from a self-development angle, I became acutely aware of how much my mood and mental state were affected by the amount of movement I did. So, when my climbing progress plateaued due to my technique outpacing my strength, it was a total no brainer that I would start training outside the wall to build up my strength. I didn't even think about it, I just wanted to do it, and so I started doing bodyweight training (calisthenics). When I first started, it was much more physically demanding than anything I did at the time. And in my logical brain I dreaded every session I went to before it started. Sometimes I didn't want to do it because I knew how tiring it was or because I wasn't as strong as others. But no matter what I felt before, ten or fifteen minutes into the session, with the instructor cheering us on, the music blaring, my adrenalin and heart pumping I felt superhuman, amazing, like I could do or achieve anything. So, each time, as I slowly reprogrammed my mindset, the fear and dread turned into energy and enthusiasm for feeling as awesome as I did after class. Next came power yoga, because I wanted to improve my flexibility and do more meditation, seeking the next level of this high.

Now if I'm not working away from home, I may joyfully and willingly exercise for 6-8 hours a week. And it has nothing to do with my weight, only knowing how great I feel for doing it both short and long term. And don't get me wrong I still sweat and curse and moan when I'm tired and in a tough session. But the simple fact that I'm doing it for my own joy and no other outcome means I never hate or resent it, and whenever I'm doing it, I want to be there. And of course, there are times when I don't want to. I choose intense forms of exercise because that's what I love, but there are times when I don't feel like doing it at all. After a heavy work stretch, I may prefer to rest. When I'm on my period I usually do nothing but walk my dogs for movement. In the summer I may prefer to do outdoor sports or laze around in the sun. Because if it's not going to bring me joy to move in a particular way, then it's simply not good for me. Going to the gym to earn your calories is just diet culture wrapped up as a lifestyle choice. Do it because you love it. And if you don't, do something that you *do* love: walk your dogs, climb a hill, take a dance class, lift weights, go trampolining. And if you do just love treadmills and rowing machines, go to the gym and have your fill!

5

TRUST YOUR GUT

I know that in my case, my connection to my intuition was so buried and ignored, when I first started to try to get my head around it, I could barely make sense of it. Ironically it was my need to make sense of everything that was holding me back from connecting to and making use of my intuition. And it's a core belief of mine that many aspects of internal work to improve our relationship with ourselves can, and should, be applied to our relationship with food. Intuition is often described as feeling your way through things rather than thinking through them. It can be a little jarring to try to quiet your brain, which is so very useful and domineering in your life and let these mystical things called feelings weigh in on decisions. And to be perfectly honest, when it comes to areas of life outside of food, I'm still working on it. Yet with food, I am all too aware of how overthinking can be the enemy but didn't connect it to this intuition malarkey until more recently. I honestly just saw it as me loving food and cooking because I could switch off and didn't need to think (which I spent the whole day doing—or more accurately, it would switch off my internal chatter which was full of judgemental meanness). Once I started doing the self-development stuff, I realised that looking in the fridge and pulling things out and just making food with love and joy, knowing it's all going to be yummy, was basically what I should try to do with my life in general. So, I promise to share what I have learnt and to also keep using it to work on being more intuitive outside of the kitchen.

When I make a decision about a meal or ingredient selection, I know instinctively that it feels right. In fact, knowing doesn't come into it, my gut makes the call. If I'm exhausted and hungry, I'll treat myself to a pizza, if it's in season I eat asparagus every day, if I want to make a curry, I just know what spices to combine to achieve the experience I want. These seemingly easy choices don't require thinking, they aren't being pulled from your head. Instead, they just well up from your centre and manifest themselves through gut-led effortless intuition. And this is much more about knowing yourself than knowing everything about ingredients or cooking techniques. These choices respond to feelings not thoughts, and true desires, not imposed standards. It's been hard (for me at least) to really connect to my intuition in other areas of life. My approach to developing this skill is to try and access the same 'force' that guides me in all things food. That certainty and faith, that multi-sensory experience, that unfailing clarity that comes when you know in your gut you've made the right choice. The one thing that occurred to me as I pondered this subject was that to me, 'intuitive eating' is just eating. Really that's what eating should be to everybody. We have so warped our relationship with food and body image that we have to redefine and reconnect to the most basic, primal gut instinct we have.

And honestly, it's when I let my logical brain get involved that

I make decisions around food that tend to be less right, or flat out wrong for me at that particular time. Takeaway choice anxiety is a good example, and I will share it because you may be thinking all this stuff only applies to eating spinach, but it doesn't. When I don't want to cook and I start to look at what I may want to order (with my brain), just like trying to find something to watch on television, I can't for the life of me make up my mind, and spend forever scrolling, previewing, menu hopping and checking ratings until I've used up the time equivalent of a feature film trying to choose. Eventually, I get so exasperated I either eat beans on toast at home, or I order my usual from my favourite local pizzeria. Now here's the rub: there are probably 3 or 4 places I regularly order takeaway from. One is pizza, another is burgers/shakes/fries, then Lebanese, and occasionally the chippy. And they are very different meals. If I acknowledged that I know myself and those options are all I ever use anyway, I wouldn't even have to think, I would just know what I wanted. Because, if you want pizza, you definitely don't want Lebanese. And fries don't hit the same spot as chippy chips. These are very intuitive and easy decisions to make, that guarantee enjoyment and satisfaction, which should be prerequisites for all of us when it comes to putting things in our mouths. But the app offers me all these choices, and there is some externally driven voice (probably advertising!) in my head telling me I should try something new, look for something that's on offer, or even not be so lazy and make myself dinner. As soon as you let the brain take over, you aren't just working with yourself and your own feelings, wants and needs. Every external force that has penetrated your psyche suddenly gets a say in your eating decisions, when they have no business doing so.

That's why I think the simple act of preparing and cooking food intuitively can be so magical—and the more you do it, the less you feel inclined to seek out a recipe to rely on instead. I know that it requires some knowledge and skill, but the skill required to make delicious everyday food is well within everyone's grasp, and the intuitive sense of how to make it work with ingredients and flavours comes with (as in life) from trying and succeeding or trying and learning from your mishaps. In a general sense, making decisions around food (or anything) without using your intuition, is for me the easiest way to miss out on the joy of it all. I'm not saying don't think your way through anything, I'm saying feel your way through it and think your way to making it a reality. My own experience has been that being more intuitive in life and with food doesn't mean being lazy or excessive, it means prioritising what I want and need through checking in with myself rather than what I think I should do or eat or be. So even though I absolutely love cake, and joke that I eat it all day every day, I actually don't (at least not regularly). It can be as simple as eating nothing but cake all day and allowing myself to feel gross, not hating myself for it, and intuitively eating an amount that leads me to feel less gross next time. Or eating the amount that makes me feel gross and knowing that it will, and not caring because if I listen to my body, it will probably want far less cake and far more vegetables the next day anyway (and if it doesn't, then it'll cope with the cake fest just fine). And equally, that applies to carbs or salad or cheese or fruit. By simply allowing yourself to notice how you feel when you eat or when you make decisions about food, accepting those feelings and decisions without judgement and knowing that they mean nothing in the long run, you can start to work with your body and its signals rather than trying to quash and dismiss them. And then you get to enjoy all the food you eat without guilt or judgement or doing it to inflict punishment on yourself.

You may wonder why I haven't gone into more detail about

'intuitive eating' specifically—but in one sense that's exactly what I'm talking about, but I just think it's so much more than that. I think the idea of slowly learning to listen to your body and eliminate guilt and self-doubt from eating choices is a really sustainable way of converging on a diet ideally suited in an individual way to each person. But it requires commitment and acceptance of potential changes in weight and body shape during the massive mindset change that has to occur. I just want to point out how perfectly that previous statement could be used to describe the journey I ended up on. The idea of learning to listen to your intuition and eliminate guilt and self-doubt from your life choices is a really sustainable way of converging on a life that is ideal for the individual (and the collective). But it requires commitment and acceptance of potentially massive changes in your lifestyle, career and relationships during the huge mindset shift that has to occur. As I said, intuitive eating is really just eating. And perhaps that's true of cooking, living, interacting, connecting intuitively too. And this is why I think intuitive eating is a bit of a minimising description for what is a lifelong and holistic practice of looking inward, loving yourself unconditionally and using your intuition as a guiding force (together with your brain) in all aspects of life and decision making.

6

EMBRACE THE UNKNOWN

Learning to deal with uncertainty has been a huge part of my self-development journey. And as I started to examine my focus on perfectionism and control, and worked on letting go of them, I realised that my approach in the kitchen was the blueprint for my success at doing these things in life more broadly. By recognising how I dealt with uncertainty well in the kitchen, and not anywhere else, I have started to be able to translate my kitchen calmness into a more philosophical, conscious and uncertainty-managing approach to life. Don't get me wrong, it's not been easy. And I still find it much easier to deal with uncertainty in the kitchen than I do in life. But I'm working on it. 'Progress not perfection' is my new mantra.

When it comes to food (and life), dealing with uncertainty is about mindset, letting go of expectations and self-love. Of course, uncertainty can be terrifying, but because it can create such a spiral of negativity, embracing it is liberating and fulfilling. In life, I try to approach uncertainty with excitement instead of fear.

They're physically very similar emotions so it's an easy switch. I do this when I get anxious about doing new things: I tell everyone around, and myself, 'I'm excited about it!' and eventually, I am! And the same can and should be true when it comes to how we see food. Trying new ingredients and dishes can be unsettling to creatures of habit that find comfort in the consistency and predictability of what they eat. So instead of ignoring or giving in to your fear of the unknown, recognise it, and work on rebranding that anxious feeling into one of excitement. It might sound stupid, but it really works. You aren't scared to try cooking without a recipe, you're excited about it. You aren't worried about trying a new dish or ingredient, it's a fun, new adventure.

I personally tend towards seeking control, and particularly when anxious or unsure, control feels like the last bastion of sovereignty in the midst of chaos. And I often feel that the way food and cooking are commercialised also encourages that tendency. I'm not saying that TV cooking shows and recipe books are bad, but they aren't the only way to go about cooking, and it's not often made that clear. 'Bish, bash, bosh'-type chefs come pretty close. But the belief that people need and want recipes to follow is a bit of a self-fulfilling prophecy, that also happens to lead to lots of book sales and TV shows. And we are comforted as consumers by having the uncertainty removed from food and cooking. We can order, buy ready-made, or find the recipe to make whatever we are conditioned to believe we should be eating, to the point that it becomes automatic and almost mindless, often joyless, and even bordering on stressful. Even as a professional chef, having to follow recipes from a page is something that sucks the joy out of the experience for me. I can't tell you how many baking recipes I have memorised when making them repeatedly at work. And a lot of them are still in there! The main reason is that

I feel like I haven't been part of the cooking process if the whole thing is controlled and dictated by a piece of paper. It makes me anxious, I feel like I don't know what I'm doing and need to keep referring to the paper (usually out of comfort, not necessity), I make the thing and at the end of it have no idea what I did or how I did it. My solution was to concentrate on the recipes, to embed them in my brain (instead of mindless recipe following), and then do away with the bits of paper and work from memory and intuition instead. And there is no way of underlining the uncertainty of an intuitive approach better than the fact that I would often make something from memory, put it in the oven and realise at that moment that I forgot a key ingredient (baking powder usually) and have no option but to wait for it to bake and see how it turns out, or admit defeat, chuck it and start again.

I'll be honest, when I first started out at work both in a corporate setting and subsequently in kitchens, this was not something I was good at. A total control freak and disproportionately affected by change and uncertainty, I spent a lot of energy trying to control things and plan for every eventuality, often wasting time catastrophising and scenario testing everything in my brain, paralysed into inaction due to fear of the unknown. Back to the missing baking powder—this is precisely how I have learnt to cope better with uncertainty in life as well as the kitchen. The key being mindset, of course! Initially, it would feel like a disaster—wasted time, ingredients, lost money, feeling like an idiot for making a basic mistake. And when it felt like that, it kept happening again and again. Something goes wrong that is a simple mistake or totally out of your control and you lose the plot, berate yourself for letting it happen, and dwell on it. And that, of course, just primes you to repeat the same experience over and over. So now my approach is to *not* beat myself up about things going wrong that I can't control or even if I just make a simple mistake. Instead of seeing it as a waste of time or product, I see it as a chance to learn something either about cooking or science (what does this recipe turn out like if you miss out a key ingredient? Have I created a magical new culinary invention?) or about myself (I have a tendency to forget baking powder) and then go on with life enriched and empowered by my learnings.

I was lucky enough to grow up in a family that loved food, came from Africa and so didn't have as much of a diet-culture tainted view of cooking and eating. As a result, I have never feared food, cooking, ingredients or new culinary experiences. I relish them all. A big part of this is the ingredients I use and how much joy they bring me. Of course, I love going to a market and touching, smelling, seeing all the stuff on offer, but I also have a particularly exciting 'shopping' experience in my life that I would highly recommend to everyone (availability dependent of course). Find a local fruit and veg box delivery company that rescues wonky and surplus produce from all over the world that would otherwise go to waste, and you'll be in intuitive cooking heaven. Each week for less than £12 at the time of writing, I get pretty much all the fruit and veg I need in a week, a mix of locally grown seasonal stuff and more exotic items rescued from further afield. It's never samey, even in the less varied offering of winter (because they rescue stuff from all over the world, I get pineapples in winter and it's all rather wonderful), so I don't get bored, and I am always excited to find out what's in the box. I even stop myself from checking the contents online when I get the email notification about it—I want to enjoy the surprise and open the box like a kid at Christmas, discovering new and wonderful things and inspiration for upcoming meals as I rifle through the contents. It's so dreamy, cost-effective and a really smart and practical way to contribute to sustainability.

There is something so engaging about cooking intuitively and without relying on recipes and rules. If you rely on your intuition and let your mind, body and soul all get a say in food-related decisions, you have no choice but to do it mindfully and consciously, and this is part of seeking the joy. It *will* be a bit stressful at first as it's out of your comfort zone. But that really is where all the good stuff is waiting for you: by definition, all the new and hitherto untapped magic you want to bring into your kitchen (and your life) is waiting in that expansive and uncertain place your ego and comfort zone completely ignore! I am in the process of writing a bigger, more detailed book which brings together intuitive cooking, self-development and my approach to having a joyful relationship with food—into one unique take on living a more intuitive life, loving food, and of course, loving yourself. So, if you like what you read here there is more to come, or for a practical approach, I run online intuitive cooking and mindset courses too!

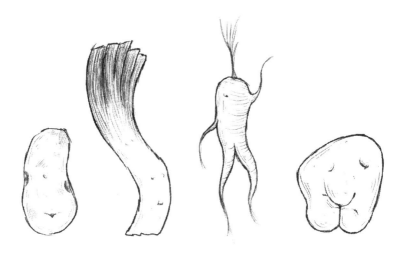

7

ENGAGE YOUR SENSES AND EMOTIONS

We are surrounded by obstacles that stop us from connecting to our food. We can buy literally everything including fresh and frozen food online, and get someone else to interpret our preferences for how ripe our fruit and veg should be. Supermarkets are full of plastic barriers that stop us from being able to properly touch or smell fresh produce—but what other way do we have to know whether something is ripe, or fresh or delicious, or suits our personal taste preferences. We can get everything prepared to whatever degree we require, from chopped onions to full-blown ready meals. On their own, these small convenient changes to the way we get food into our kitchens may seem like lifesavers. But if you take it to an extreme, for me, it's one of the greatest sources of disconnect from food. You can order everything online, all pre-prepared or ready-made, and not touch or smell or prepare or taste anything, yet still have a meal at the end of it. And yes, it's still food, it provides nutrition and will do the physical things that food is meant to do. But you miss out on the world of sensory, emotional and spiritual pleasure that food offers, and even worse, you programme yourself to accept that as a way of life. This limits food to its most basic and necessary form, as a functional requirement and nothing more.

Having a relationship with food is something quite different—it's a two-way street. If we are talking about dictionary definitions, a relationship is the way in which things or people are connected or the way in which things behave towards each other. I definitely see food in this way, as something I have a connection to and where there is a two-way flow of energy, and massive potential for contributing to my wellbeing. Food also provides a connection to other people, socially and energetically, that transcends all barriers. It's a hugely powerful and emotional thing when you start to look at it from a different perspective and have the desire to have a productive and fulfilling relationship with food rather than living in conflict with or fear of it. Take cooking and eating socially. As an extension of you, your energy and your love, the food you cook has immense power to reach people on levels that you may not normally be able to. Food has the power to make an event something people will never forget and can bring people from disparate familial and friendship groups together with ease. It's no coincidence that feasting is a cross-cultural feature of big celebrations—what on earth would your third cousin say to your uncle-in-law at your wedding, if not something about how amazing (or otherwise) the food is. Food has no language barrier, no generational gap. And despite how different food cultures and cuisines can be, the fact that food is used as a social and celebratory activity is a universal truth—and in a world of division, difference and competition, it's these simple, primal things we all share that can help to ground our experience in what's really important and gives us the most joy.

Food is a form of emotional expression as well as connection. I often feel a little socially awkward, but I know that I have food as the language of love, joy, condolence, comfort, celebration, apology or to bridge age and experience gaps. I have a cake, bake, bread, preserve, curry, and fried snack for every situation. My nephew's first taste of sourdough was a loaf made by me. I can claim that honour, knowing how much amazing food there is ahead of him and wanting to be part of that journey of discovery and joy. This is what sharing food and cooking for others is about. There is no clearer form of energetic transfer in our everyday lives. It may seem cliché to say that love is the secret ingredient that makes the difference when it comes to cooking amazing food. But clichés exist for a reason. It's no surprise that people who hate cooking aren't usually the best cooks and don't like the food that they make. And even if the food that they make doesn't taste perfect or exactly as they intended, people who love cooking and transfer that love to what they prepare simply take mistakes in the kitchen as an opportunity for evolution. You may want to punch me right now—I get it, I've been there.

Even the simplest of home-cooked meals can offer that sort of energetic transfer—if it's made with love it feeds with love too. That's the magic of food that we all know to be true but are tricked into seeing as silly or unnecessary to life—if we don't keep food as an active and evolving part of our human experience. I can't help myself here: how much love, care, joy and high-frequency energy do you think a factory processed plastic packed ready meal has, one that has been clinically moved by machines and lasers never to make contact with a human until it goes into a mouth? And you can transfer all sorts of emotion too, just like any other energetic transfer, bad vibes flow just as forcefully as good ones (if not more so). And because what we eat is a huge part of our self-care, it can be amazing, but can also be so damaging if we work with the wrong energetic flow. I love cooking and eating, and see them as cathartic, therapeutic activities. But if I am in a funk of some sort for any reason, I become less inclined to cook, eat properly or generally look after myself. I ignore or stop experiencing hunger signals, which in turn makes me less rational and more irritable, then I am unproductive and get even more annoyed and before I know it I have wished an entire day away, stuck in my head unable to offer myself even the most basic self-care. Yet because I have a relationship with food, it basically becomes my yardstick to assess the state of my general wellbeing. It can be an indication of a disconnect in my mind, body, soul complex that needs addressing. Because when I'm living my best life, my relationship with food is vital, active and joyful. And the same is true, in my opinion, for everyone, and is valid for our relationship with food and with ourselves. Anxiety, fear, inaction, 'should' mentalities are all a symptom of misalignment, not of failure. So, if you find yourself frustrated and hating yourself or your body over what you eat, reflect on what the emotional or spiritual disconnect is that is leading you to treat yourself or your body without kindness, don't just assume you're an incompetent human. Emotional eating isn't a problem as much as emotional problems are. What I mean here is that on the face of it, the fact that chocolate can make you feel better when you're sad is absolutely awesome. But if you're eating chocolate all the time, because you're sad all the time, it's not the chocolate that's the issue—it's the constant sadness that you avoid processing by eating chocolate compulsively. And processing and engaging with our emotions means emotional eating isn't a substitute for dealing with our feelings, it just provides comfort and support while we do. Sit with your emotions, process them, feel them and then accept that they don't define you. You don't have to react to or act upon them—eat a piece of chocolate, offer yourself some kindness instead of judgement over it and see if that changes anything. This combined with a non-restrictive and abundant approach to food is so powerful in reprogramming your mindset and body to the reality of food today.

And because mindset is such a crucial part of our experience, working on it can be really powerful in all areas of life. Of course, food is my focus here so I will stick to it. And now in particular (2020 coronavirus pandemic in full force at the time of writing), with enforced isolation and time on our increasingly bored and lonely hands, there is an opportunity to challenge and develop our (food) mindset. That familiar phrase of 'I don't have time to cook'—is something that is increasingly less true. Sure, time is required to prepare food, and certainly cooking in an everyday sense is more time than skill intensive. I understand that when you are living and working in a mad rat race, juggling responsibilities and demands and ambitions and dreams, cooking can seem like a waste of time. But given that I see cooking and eating as on a par with meditation and yoga, I'll roll out another infuriatingly true statement: if you think you haven't got the time to meditate (or cook, or rest, or play), you probably need to do it for twice as long. In the quest for mindfulness, presence and a more conscious human experience, I don't think there is such a thing as too much of a good thing. So just like yoga, or meditation, or walking in nature, cooking and enjoying food can form a core part of your wellness, self-care and mindfulness practice. And if you acknowledge its power and elevate it to that status, then you can get the same kind of peace and release from preparing dinner as you do from a yoga class or guided candlelit meditation. As I said, this is all mindset. On the face of it, peeling potatoes is peeling potatoes. And you can be annoyed by it because you see it as a waste of time that you could use for something else 'productive' (even though cooking *is* productive) or you could enjoy it and get some benefit from it. You just need to reframe the way you see it and connect to it emotionally—enjoy (even be grateful) that you have a moment of calm where your mind is free from stimulation and demand. It's a moment to stop, breath and engage in something unchallenging but sensory, that focuses you on the present moment. It's literally a form of yoga if you choose to see it that way. It's magic!

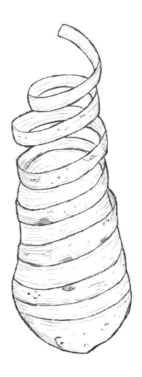

8

BE GRATEFUL

It's no secret that gratitude can make a huge difference to your life, your sense of wellbeing and your mindset. And this applies to food as well as the rest of it. In particular, it's much harder to feel lack and insufficiency if you acknowledge and really appreciate everything that you already have. And sure, it's easy to be grateful for sunshine, puppies, falling in love or buying your dream home. But the real magic comes when you can learn to be grateful for, or appreciate, everything good and bad that life throws your way (I like using 'appreciate' as it feels more appropriate when you aren't just talking about roses and fairies). Being grateful for things you would normally deem a failure or stroke of bad luck is really key to raising your energetic level both in life and when it comes to your relationship with food. Then there is no failure, only a lesson. There is no annoyance, just an exercise in patience. Someone didn't hurt you; they exposed a trigger you can work on. Food is not your enemy, it's the fuel you need to be the awesome person you are.

Experience taught me the hard way that saying or writing down things you are grateful for is quite different to actually feeling grateful or appreciative of a thing, person or experience. When I was told that gratitude was going to fix all my problems, I thought all I needed to do was write down anything vaguely good in my life on a gratitude list every day and sit back and watch the magic happen. As it turns out, it doesn't quite work that way—you actually have to *feel* grateful (at which point writing it down stops mattering nearly as much). So, it took me a while to get to grips with gratitude, because I lean to thinking my feelings rather than feeling them. In the end, for me, it was a few spontaneous moments of real gratitude for amazing things that happened in my life combined with this increased awareness and desire to connect to it that got me into the swing of connecting a feeling to that word, 'grateful'. Cue the magic.

One place where it is easy to start and important to be grateful is in those areas of our life or things or people we take for granted. Not only is the everyday food we eat a perfect example of this, practising gratitude and appreciation when it comes to food can promote positive emotions and self-talk over negative versions (which is useful for your mindset outside of food too). It is so rare that we really appreciate how lucky we are to have all the diversity and deliciousness that our modern, globalised food production has to offer. So much variety, freshness, convenience and nourishment at our fingertips without even having to think about it. Pretty amazing, right? And that's just a standalone assessment, no relative comparison to anyone else. Gratitude also takes the fight out of it—you can't simultaneously beat yourself up for what you're eating and be grateful for it. So, choose the love and kindness over the fear and anger even when you indulge or make choices out of convenience.

This is particularly important when it comes to foods you would normally deem to be 'naughty' or 'unhealthy' or 'dirty', as this is often where people are the least kind to themselves. Firstly, we don't attach moral value to food anymore, do we? Sure, they aren't going to be great as a permanent dietary solution, but convenient, indulgent and processed foods still offer pleasure, joy and save you time—we can all agree on that. It's diet culture and subconscious conditioning that create negative stories and self-hatred around occasionally consuming those things. So, let's see and appreciate them for what they are: convenient, tasty, pleasurable parts of our human experience. The idea of convenience and processed foods isn't evil (flour still is a processed food, for example). OK, so they are not always the pinnacle of food made with love that eats with love, as I already mentioned. And sure, the ingredients and marketing that lie behind a lot of modern mass-produced convenience food are not something I agree with, but that's on the companies that produce them, not the concept of cake as a delicious and life-affirming food or grab and go lunches to keep us going through our demanding work days. In reality, some convenience foods are nutritious whilst some are less so, but there is so much stigma about things like sugar and flour (hey diet culture!) that we feel judged (well, we judge ourselves) for eating them. This is much harder to do if you are actively appreciating that ready-made sandwich for exactly what it is, and not judging yourself for what external forces have made you believe it says about your moral virtue.

Another benefit of practising gratitude when it comes to food is that it naturally increases your emotional and sensory engagement with what you're cooking and/or eating. It makes your food choices more mindful and conscious and frames them with positivity and joy (hating and speaking unkindly to yourself about your food choices or stressing about having to cook has got to be worse for your mental and physical health than the odd bit of cake or takeaway). Be grateful that you can order in when you want to, and at the same time, appreciate the opportunity to slow down and engage in a task when you do prepare a meal. As with so many of the topics in this book, it's about mindset. You can completely change your relationship with food and cooking by working on the internal chatter you have. If feelings of stress and resentment creep in when you have to cook a meal, work on reframing it in your head with appreciation: it's a mindful moment of quiet, you don't have to be a master chef to make something tasty, you're cooking for yourself (and maybe your friends or family), and you will all feel awesome after a lovingly prepared meal that you sit and eat together, you can spend some quality time with your kids in the kitchen. It will seem alien and forced at first, but as with all mindset work, it's about reprogramming on repeat to replace old thought patterns with new ones that serve you better.

9

DON'T JUDGE YOURSELF (OR OTHERS)

I've alluded to this quite frequently throughout this book, but I think it's so important that it deserves its own focus. Being judgemental and unkind is frankly exhausting, whether directed at someone else or at yourself. And I believe that being kind to yourself and letting go of judgement are two of the most important factors in having a joyful relationship with food. For so many people (including myself until very recently), it's not even something on the radar. Firstly, it's pretty uncomfortable to actually listen to your inner critic and the things you say to yourself, and even more uncomfortable to try and change that voice to offer positivity, encouragement and kindness. So, we blissfully go through life without giving it conscious consideration, it's just the voice in our heads and we can't do anything about it.

We may go through the day telling ourselves off for everything, choosing to pick out negatives and failures rather than acknowledge our achievements and successes, or even the lessons we can learn from our setbacks. You may be like me and feel weird and awkward when you first have to look at how you speak to yourself and want to shrug it off as silly nonsense. And when it comes to food, it's so easy to do because the world is full of inspiration for ways for us to be nasty to ourselves and judge our every choice and behaviour. But once you start to be aware of your internal monologue, then gently work to change its tone, it can have a powerful effect on your mindset and overall wellbeing.

Part of all of this mindset stuff is about focusing our efforts on things that we *can* change and that have a meaningful effect on our wellbeing, whilst recognising and letting go of the things we have no control over and that are external to our core experience. And the way we speak to or about ourselves and others is absolutely something we have the capacity to change and are fully in control of—if we choose to be. It may not always seem that way, but we choose our thoughts. You choose to compare your food choices negatively against social media propaganda, and you can choose not to. You can choose not to compare anything in your life against what are very likely to be carefully curated and unrealistic ideals. The only person saying mean things inside your head is you, and you will end up not liking yourself very much if you carry on doing it. That's what happened to me. To begin with, it seemed frankly ridiculous that I would say nice, supportive things to myself in my head. So, my first step was to stop the meanness. Sure, full-blown self-love was a little out of my reach, but stopping the constant self-hatred was crucial to getting me out of my own way. It's not easy if you are used to being awful to yourself, and it will definitely feel uncomfortable and pointless, to begin with. But just as you should treat others as you would like to be treated yourself, you should treat yourself in the way you want to treat other people too.

When it comes to food, that means not passing moral

judgement on your body or food choices (or on anyone else's). It's not just what you eat, it's where it comes from and who makes it. It's OK not to be the perfect citizen when it comes to food. What's not OK is to hate yourself for it. Because like any petulant child will tell you, making the right choices is psychologically hard to come to terms with when someone is constantly nagging at you to do it and then waiting to tell you off for not doing it well enough. So don't make it hard on yourself. Treat yourself with kindness when you take understandable shortcuts in getting food into yourself. And don't make the 'right choices' the enemy by berating and punishing yourself for not always making them. Similarly, when you make decisions to eat healthy, nourishing, wholesome things, don't frame them with moral or relative judgement. Because even when you do make nutritious choices, the pitfall of comparison means you never feel like your good food choices are good enough. So you even judge yourself for doing the 'right' things, because there is always an example of someone online who is doing more and better 'right' things than you are, and if you aren't doing as well as them then you are failing. Sound familiar?

Judgement is also the enemy of doing anything more intuitively. If you expect perfection or attainment of specific expectations from your relationship with food and judge yourself (and potentially others too) against those ideals, then you will likely always be disappointed. You cannot make intuitive decisions and stick with them if you are prone to second-guessing and judging yourself. It takes time and freedom to have an intuitive relationship with food—you need to work with your mind, body and soul, look inward, take notice of how certain foods and choices make you feel physically, emotionally and spiritually. Treat yourself with kindness when you test the boundaries of these aspects of your relationship with food, knowing that they provide valuable information and experience that you can trust your body to use wisely—if you let it.

My journey with eating meat has been a recent area of my relationship with food that has needed some judgement focused mindset work. Until sometime early in 2018, I was an eater of everything. No allergies (well I'm allergic to cartilaginous fish but how much do I lose out by not being able to eat shark?), no major dislikes (just red offal, still can't go there), a lover of new experiences and culinary adventures—an omnivore if ever there was one. I have this amazing barbecue, a country full of amazing farmers and a city with incredible butchers and have always prioritised quality and experience in my food. So, as a grown-up meat-eating person, I ended up eating incredible meat—infrequently. Yet it didn't actually occur to me to stop eating meat. I loved it and didn't eat it that often, I felt ethically OK about my decisions. Then one day I definitely overdid it at a burger joint, and the following day I felt awful (spoiler alert, this also coincided with my broader more general spiritual awakening and efforts to reconnect to my intuition). That day, I decided I wouldn't eat meat anymore, because of how I felt, and it occurred to me that every time I ate meat, what I experienced was just another version of feeling as gross as I did on that particular occasion, with varying severity. And I didn't eat any meat at all for over a year—I felt amazing, physically fitter and stronger than ever, I noticed far more obvious gains from all the exercise I was doing. I will admit that I became a bit smug about my vegetarianism. I will also admit that I started to judge others for what I deemed to be excessive meat-eating and judge myself when I had those inevitable and aforementioned cheeseburger cravings (I was restricting my diet arbitrarily, which we know from Chapter 2 is not helpful).

My high horse became a little precarious as I became

consumed with cravings for burgers that I had never experienced before. But being stubborn and judgemental, I stuck to it until I came to my senses about what my relationship with food meant to me and sorted out my mindset. On that trip to New York, I managed to reprioritise and remember that joy and love and yumminess are the best yardsticks for food and for life. I went with my gut instinct: 'That barbecue looks tasty, the joy of eating it is more than the discomfort my stomach will feel'. And that week was the week I got back to myself regarding how I see food. I stopped being a vegetarian. I still don't really eat meat though. I just stopped restricting my diet and providing an area of my eating that I could focus judgement and comparison on. So most of the time I choose not to eat meat. Sometimes choose the opposite. But whichever I do, it's because I want to, and because it feels right, and there is no random external rule or restriction that gets a look in. Most importantly I don't judge myself for it either way and nor do I judge others for their personal choices. As I said, on the face of it I am basically a vegetarian. But this way if I choose to eat meat there is no guilt or shame or judgement attached to it, within or without.

I feel like talking about judgement puts a super heavy and effortful vibe onto the work, but really it's about being gentle and kind to yourself. Let yourself make decisions that honour your feelings and needs, and gently encourage yourself to make time for the foods and choices that make you feel great, and don't impose arbitrary rules and comparisons that provide fuel to your judgement fire. Then decisions and choices around food can be made with joy instead of from the sense of being backed into a corner (by yourself or anyone else).

10

HAVE FUN

There's no reason why food choices and cooking should cause stress and anxiety, be a chore or something you want to avoid. A lot of traditional food culture has been co-opted by capitalism and consumerism and we have lost the time and value attributed to our relationship with food in the past, having been conditioned to prioritise other things (and the convenience foods sweep in to save the day). But a shared love of food and cooking between friends and family is *the* way to turn it from stressful drudgery to mindful, life-affirming fun. Cooking is a big part of my job, and I *still* find it fun—I think because I approach it mindfully and have been lucky enough to have had food and cooking at the core of my social, familial, emotional and spiritual experience from the get-go. And, like a broken record going on about mindset, here it is again: a joyful approach and mindset towards food is basically fundamental and non-negotiable in the pursuit of a joyful relationship with food. You get out what you put in.

A huge part of my own personal food-related fun derives from the social and family aspect of cooking and eating. And let me be clear, I'm not just talking about entire days spent in the kitchen preparing food (although that is included). I'm talking about every aspect of our relationship with food: shopping, cooking and baking together, eating together, trying new restaurants or revisiting our old favourites—these are the experiences that form my love of food and they are all more fun with other people involved. I love cooking and baking on my own, but I enjoy it even more with someone else, if the end product is destined for sharing or to be given as a gift to someone. It's a channel for all the love and energy you want to embody and transfer. And because sharing food experiences is a pretty ubiquitous social activity, it's a great place to start dialling up that fun factor. But that transfer of energy and love is also why it's a really wonderful act of self-care to approach food and cooking this way even if it is just for yourself. I get it, because I have been there, and continue to go there on occasion—cooking for one can seem a little pointless. Why bother spending a lot of time just cooking for yourself, right? Well, I'm hoping that the content of this book may be starting to change that mindset...

Let's assume for a moment that what you have read so far has resonated with you (I mean you stuck with me, didn't you?). So we agree that our relationship with food is massively important to our wellbeing: mind, body and soul. We agree that mindset is key to having a joyful relationship with food. We agree that by seeing our connection to food as an active and evolving relationship we can use it as a soul-filling, life-affirming, vitalising part of our self-love and self-care. So, we can agree that we want to honour this connection to food, and our personal connection to it is arguably the most important area to try and foster a new relationship based on love and joy. In which case, taking yourself out for dinner or preparing yourself a carefully and lovingly cooked meal isn't weird or awkward or self-indulgent, it's just wonderful.

As a first step, nostalgia is a good place to look to start getting your joy back in the kitchen. We all have a few childhood memories of baking with loved ones and licking bowls clean of their cake mix dregs. For me, two specific ones always spring to mind and I'm surprised to say neither of them involves cake or sugar or dessert (I am honestly shocked). First is scrambling eggs at the weekend for breakfast with my family. My sister and I used to fight over who got to make them and me being about two feet tall aged seven, would have to grab a chair to stand on so I could tower over the pan and stir the eggs. And I would constantly ask my mum for tips and instructions and scientific commentary on the entire egg scrambling process. And every time I make scrambled eggs at home, such a simple and quick meal (I regularly eat breakfast for dinner, it's something I really love to do), I am filled with all this nostalgia and comfort like a seven-year-old standing on a chair asking my mum if my eggs are perfect. The second is making chapatis with my grandmother on a Friday afternoon ahead of our big weekly family dinner. She is, and always has been, some sort of wizard in the kitchen. We used to help her roll the dough out, on her special round stands with her little funny-shaped wooden rolling pins. And ours would be misshapen and hers would be perfect and take seconds to roll. And she would cook them all and let us eat our wonky ones covered in butter, sometimes with sugar. Oh phew, there's the sugar. If you set about cooking something you know you love to eat and remember fondly from childhood you've hooked yourself up with a joy reserve before you even get into the kitchen, to help you resist the pull to stress and anxiety. And whilst you may not be able to bake fairy cakes and jam tarts every day, introducing fun-filled kitchen experiences into your life is all part of that mindset and programming change to redefine the way you see these activities and experiences.

Turning back to dealing explicitly with the everyday food choices and cooking tasks that can sometimes be categorised as pointless or not worth spending time over. Just like cooking up a nostalgic childhood treat is about love and memory and social bonds, and eating it makes us feel good, happy and connected to others—as a solo act of self-care, it requires a love of and connection to self that a lot of people dismiss as folly. It's about loving yourself enough to feed, nourish and treat yourself in the way you would your partner or children or best friend. Anything can be fun and useful if you can frame it as an exercise in mindfulness and self-care. And sure it may not be the laugh a minute raucous fun of a party with your mates, but I still have fun making myself a meal in an empty house—my favourite tunes on as loud as the dogs can handle, a cup of tea in my favourite mug, time to myself to mindfully enjoy mindless tasks like chopping and stirring, a sensory ride with the smells filling the kitchen and my appetite growing as it takes in all the aromas and tastes that await me. And something delicious to eat at the end of it all too. As per, it's all about mindset.

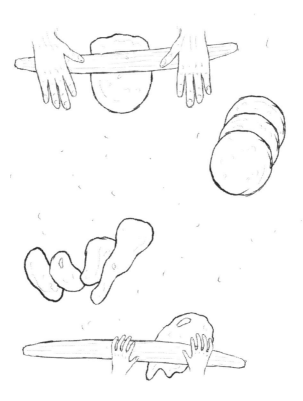

FINAL THOUGHTS

Having a joyful relationship with food starts in large part with your relationship with yourself. I've said it before, a lot, so I'll say it again—it's your mindset. OK, so it's a little more than that. It's using the combination of your mindset and connecting with your body and intuition to forge your own personal, joyful connection with food: cooking it, eating it, choosing ingredients or items from a menu, preparing, sharing, even remembering it.

There may still be a part of you resisting or dismissing all this as hippy weirdo New Age rubbish. Or you may think of it as the privilege of a rich and idle few. But ask yourself if that could be part of this 'Diet Culture X Capitalism' conditioning I've been talking about. Food transcends all boundaries you can think of: a connection to food and availability of fresh produce are on offer to a lot of us if we seek out the ways we are able to achieve them and don't try to measure them using standards and metrics that come from the very culture we are trying to shake off. Having access to a multitude of whole and unprocessed foods and every cuisine under the sun, for example, aren't a requirement for having a joyful relationship with food. Nor is curating your every eating habit to limit your calorie intake below a specific level (usually the level you need to sustain yourself in life, I might add). Nor is never eating carbs or sugar.

And I'm not minimising the work that's involved, the resistance that comes up and the ingrained conditioning at play. It's exhausting just thinking about it. But it's this work that liberates you from your fear and anxiety and brings you back to a point of trusting yourself and your intuition. Speaking from experience and ongoing struggle, it's a matter of prioritisation and commitment to doing the hard and uncomfortable things that are required to reprogram yourself towards knowing what is good for you, mind, body and soul—and no longer relying on someone else to decide for you.

Having been on the receiving end of this in a different context, I know how triggering it can be, but I also know that those are usually the areas of fear where the work is most needed and useful, especially when joy is on the other side of it—and you never know what magic could result from it. You may discover new things about yourself, new fruits or vegetables that you love, new dishes or meals that both taste great and make you feel vital and energised. You may find a new greengrocer where you can explore fresh produce, buy just what you need and learn about seasonality as you shop. You might start using a produce delivery service (it doesn't even have to be weekly to start with!) and having adventurous, intuitive cooking experiences at home (and I'm currently designing an online course just for you!). You might stop telling yourself off when you fancy a cheeky takeaway or need to snack between meals because you're hungry. You might find a moment of peace and mindfulness in the kitchen or a fun way to spend time with your family and friends. And I hope you do!

A BIT MORE ABOUT ME

I specialise in an intuitive approach to food and cooking. It's about sharing the love that comes from having a mindful and intuitive relationship with what we eat—buying ingredients, preparing and cooking them with joy—as well as delicious eating, of course. Having started working life as a management consultant, my path to becoming a chef and now also teacher, writer and speaker has been as much about self-development and self-love as it has been about loving food—and it's that journey that inspires what I do now. You can find out more at my lovely website www.thefoodwitch.com where you'll find great free resources and information about working with me either one-to-one or by attending my online workshops and courses or in-person retreats.

And if you liked the book and would like to support me and my work, please tell your friends and family and spread the word, the love and the joy of food! Rather than just sending them straight to Amazon to buy a copy, please direct them to my website: www.thefoodwitch.com where this book is available in multiple formats and they can find out even more about what I do!

You can also leave me a review on Amazon, Facebook or post about me on Instagram @foodwitchsal!

If you want to know more about my talented illustrator, Harry, check out his Instagram page @hazzabird or email hazzatatts@gmail.com.

Thank you!

Printed in Great Britain
by Amazon